Our Colorful Multilingual Adventure Circle Time Fun!!

Amora Santiago

Meet The Author

Hi Everybody!!!

My name is Amora and I have created this book to help introduce you to some of the basics of different languages. Being Multilingual has so many benefits that will take you very far in life. Our world is made up of so many amazing people! It's time to learn your neighbors language. Nelson Mandela quoted, "If you speak to a man in a language he understands, that goes to his head. If you talk to him in his language, that goes to his heart. I want to help you connect with many hearts.. ♥

Visit our Youtube Channel
Multilingual Stars Academy and start learning different languages with me and my family today!!!!

Meet the Family!!

Learn A Language 4 Fun, LLC

"Learning is a treasure that will follow its owner everywhere."
Chinese proverb

Fun Facts!!

1. Russian is the 8th most spoken language.

2. There are 21 countries that have Spanish as the official language.

3. Swahili is one of the most widely spoken languages in Africa.

4. German entrepreneur Hans Riegel invented gummy bears in the 1920s.

5. French is the only language taught in every country.

6. 1.2 billion people speak some form of Chinese.

7. You can play a live human chess game in Marostica, Italy in September.

8. Brazil has 60% of the rainforests that make up the Amazon rain forests.

Fun Facts!!

9. The Medu Neter is one of humanities oldest languages.

10. Latin is the basis for all the Romance languages.

11. **Arabic became a United Nations official working language on December 18, 1973.**

12. **The Samoan language is one of the oldest forms of Polynesian still in existence today.**

13. Hindi became the official language of India in 1965.

14. The Beautiful Cherry Blossom is the national flower of Japan.

15. Haiti ultimately won independence from France and thereby became the first country to be founded by former slaves.

FunFacts!!

16. Vietnam is ranked 16th worldwide in biological diversity and home to over 200 species of fish.

17. Indonesia has the largest Muslim population in the world.

18. Being a Teacher is one of the most prestigious and well-paying jobs in South Korea.

19. **Thailand is sometimes known as the "land of the smiles" because the people are apart of a peace loving culture.**

20. Persian is spoken in Iran where Beautiful Rugs have been woven for over 2,500 years.

21. In Hong Kong eating noodles on your birthday can contribute to a long and blessed life.

22. Malaysia is home to the largest individual flower in the world called Rafflesia arnoldii or corpse flower.

FunFacts!!

23. Greece is one of the sunniest countries in the world.

24. The Philippine eagle or monkey-eating eagle is considered one of the rarest and most powerful birds in the world.

25. Braille is a method of reading and writing for the blind or visually impaired.

26. Morse code is a type of code that is used to send telegraphic information using rhythm.

27. Roman numerals are a numeral system that was used by ancient Rome.

28. Hebrew is one of the original languages of the Bible.

Russian

Good Morning

Доброе утро

(doh-brreh-oo-trrah)

Good Afternoon

Добрый день

(doh-brreh- D-N)

Good Evening

Добрый вечер

(doh-brreh- V-yeh-cheh)

Spanish

¡Mucho Gusto!

(moo-choh- guu-stoh)

Its nice to meet you!

The Spring/ La Primavera

(lah-pree-mah-veh-rah)

El Otoño/The Fall!

(ehl-oh-tone-yoh)

El Invierno/The Winter

(ehl-een-B-air-noh)

El Verano /The Summer

(ehl-veh-rah-noh)

!El Gusto es mío!

(L-guu-stoh- ehs-me-oh)

Its nice to meet you to!

Swahili

Samahani, Hii ni pesa ngapi?

(sah-mah-hah-knee) (he-knee-peh-sah-nn-gah-P)

Excuse me, How much is this?

Moja is 1 **(moh-jah)**

Mbili is 2 **(mm-bee-lee)**

Tatu is 3 **(tah-2)**

Nne is 4 **(nn-neh)**

Tano is 5 **(tah-no)**

German

Wie heißen Sie?

(V-high-sen-Z)

What is your name?

Ich heiße...

(ehc -Hi-sah)

I am called...

Haitian Creole

Bonjou
Hello

Kijan ou rele?
What is your name?

Mwen rele...
My name is...

French

Les Jours de la Semaine
The days of the week

Lundi, Monday

(lon-dee)

Mardi, Tuesday

(marc-dee)

Mercredi, Wednesday

(merc-reh-dee)

**Jeudi, Thursday**

(jjuuh-dee)

Vendredi, Friday

(vohn-cruh-dee)

**Samedi, Saturday**

(sahm-dee)

Dimanche, Sunday

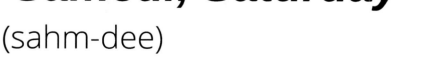(Dee-mahn-chh)

Mandarin Chinese

Nǐ de diànhuà hàomǎ shì duōshao?

(knee duh d-n-who-wah how-mah suure do-wah-shah

Your telephone number is what?

0 *líng* (lee-ng)

1 *yī* (ee)

2 *èr* (Arr)

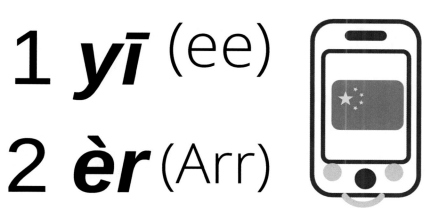

3 *sān* (SahN)

4 *sì* (Sssuh)

5 wǔ (Wooo)

Medu Neter

iiti m htp.

(e-e-t m - heh-tehp)

Welcome in Peace

ptr rn.K?(m)

(P-tah- reh-kneek)

ptr rn.T?(f)

(P-tah reh-kneech)

What is your name?

rn.i...

(reh-knee)

My name is...

Arabic

Marhaban مرحباً

(mahr-ha-bahn)

Hello

Kayfa halouka(m)?

(K-fah ha-lou-kah)

كيف حالكَ؟

Kayfa halouki(f)?

(K-fah ha-lou-key)

كيف حالك؟

How are you?

Latin

Salvete!
(sahl-weh-teh)

Hello Everyone!

Quod est tibi nomen?

(kwahd- ehst- T-B -noh-men)

What is your name?

1 *Ūnus* (oo-nohs)

 2 *duo* (do-oh)

3 *Trēs* (trehs)

4 *quattuor* (kwah-twahr)

5 *quinque* (kween-kweh)

Samoan

Tālofa, ʻO ā mai ʻoe?

(tah-loh-fah, oh-ah-ee-mah-e-oh-e)

Hello, How are you?

Samoan

SamaSama	**Viole**
(sah-mah-sah-mah)	**(V-oh-leh)**
Yellow	Purple
Mumu	**Moli**
(moo-moo)	**(moh-lee)**
Red	Orange
Moana	**Meamata**
(moh-ah-nah)	**(meh-ah-mah-tah)**
Blue	Green

Braille Alphabet

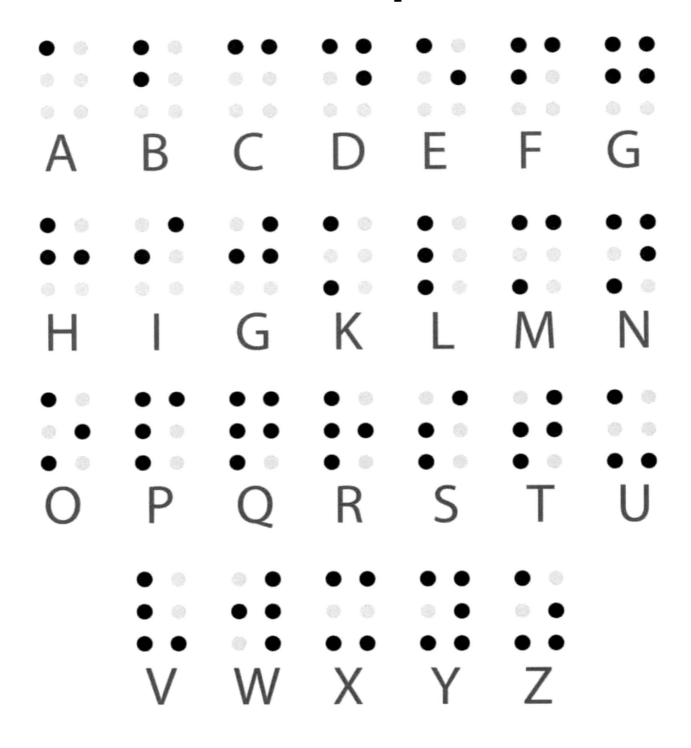

Spanish Song

¡Hola ¿Cómo estás hoy?
How are you today?
Bien, ¿y tú? Fine and you?
How are you today?
Date la Vuelta, Turnaround
How are you today?
Arriba up, *Abajo* down
Marcha Marcha Stomp your feet!
How are you today?
¡Hola ¿Cómo estás hoy?
How are you today?
Sientate Sit down, *Levantate* Stand up,
Den Palmitas, clap your hands
¡Hola ¿Cómo estás hoy?
How are you today?

Hindi

एक 1 (ek)

दो 2 (doy)

तीन 3 (teen)

चार 4 (char)

पांच 5 (pahnch)

Indonesian

Halo Selamat Siang. Nama Saya..
(Hah-loh seh-lah-maht see-ahng Nah-ma Sah-yah)

Hello Good Day, My name is..

Satu 1 (sah-2)

Dua 2 (do-wah)

Tiga 3 (T-gah)

Empat 4 (ehm-paht)

Lima 5 (lee-mah)

Greek

A α alpha,   B β beta,
Γ Υ gamma,   Δ δ delta,
E ε epsilon,   Z ζ zeta,
H η eta,   Θ θ theta
I ι iota,   K κ kappa,
Λ λ lambda,   M μ mu,
N ν nu,   Ξ ξ ksi, 1
O o omicron,   Π π pi,
P ρ rho,   Σ σς sigma
T τ tau,   Υ υ upsilon,
Φ φ phi,   X χ chi,
Ψ ψ psi,   Ω ω omega

German

Halo Gutan Tag, Meine Nummer ist..

(hah-low guu-tahn tahg)   (my-nah new-mer -Est)

Hello Good day, My number is..

1 is Eins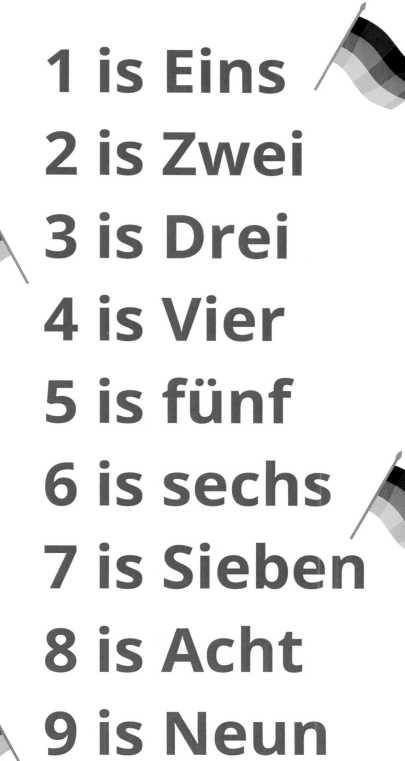
2 is Zwei
3 is Drei
4 is Vier
5 is fünf
6 is sechs
7 is Sieben
8 is Acht
9 is Neun
10 is Zehn

Roman Numerals

0	.	10	X
1	I	20	XX
2	II	30	XXX
3	III	40	XL
4	IV	50	L
5	V	60	LX
6	VI	70	LXX
7	VII	80	LXXX
8	VIII	90	XC
9	IX	100	C
		500	D
		1000	M

Vietnamese

Xin chào
(seen -chow)

Hello

1 **Môt** (moht)

2 **hai** (hiiiii)

3 **ba** (baaa)

4 **bốn** (bohn)

5 **năm** (naaahm)

Indonesian

Hari apa sekarang?

(hah-ree ah-pah seh-kah-rahng

What day is it?

- **Hari Minggu (Sunday)**

  (hah-ree - meen-guu)

- **Hari Senin (Monday)**

  (hah-ree - seh-nen)

- **Hari Selasa (Tuesday)**

  (hah-ree - sel-lah-sah)

- **Hari Rabu (Wednesday)**

  (hah-ree - rah-boo)

- **Hari Kamis (Thursday)**

  (hah-ree - kah-mees)

- **Hari Jum'at (Friday)**

  (hah-ree - juum-aht)

- **Hari Sabtu (Saturday)**

  (hah-ree - sahb-2)

Korean

몇 시예요?

(myoshi-eyo)

What time is it?

한 시 = 1 o'clock

(hansi)

두 시 = 2 o'clock

(dooshi)

세 시 = 3 o'clock

(seshi)

네 시 = 4 o'clock

(neshi)

Thai

วันจันทร์
wān-jān

Monday

วันอังคาร
wān-aāg-khāan

Tuesday

วันพุธ
wān-phóot

Wednesday

วันพฤหัส
wān-phá-réu-hàt

Thursday

วันศุกร์
wān-sòok

Friday

วันเสาร์
wān-sǎo

Saturday

วันอาทิตย์
wān-aā-thít

Sunday

Chinese

Wǒ xǐ huān...
I like...

Orange
chéngsè

橙色

Red
hóngsè

红色

蓝色
Yellow
huángsè

黄色
Blue
lánsè

绿色
Green
lǜsè

紫色
zǐsè
purple

Malay

(mah-lay

(slah- maht pah-gee)

Selamat Pagi
Good morning

Selamat tengahari
Good Afternoon

Selamat petang
Good evening

Persian

zard (Yellow)	زرد
sefīd(White)	سفيد
sūratī(Pink)	صورتى
qermez(Red)	قرمز
nāranjī(Orange)	نارنجى
sabz(Green)	سبز
ābī(Blue)	ابی
banafsh(Violet)	بنفش

Cantonese

1 一 yēd

2 二 yǐ

3 三 sām

4 四 séi

5 五 ng

Hindi

Head (Sir) सिर

Eyes (Aankh) आंखें

Shoulder (Kandha) कन्धा

Ear (Kaan) कान

Knee (Ghutana) घुटना

Nose (Naak) नाक

Mouth (Munh) मुंह

Foot (Pair) पैर

Brazilian Portuguese

Oi
(oh-ee)

Hello

O meu número é..
(oo-meh-oo- new-meh-roh- eh)

My Number is..

Um 1 (uum)

Dois 2 (doy-ees)

Três 3 (trr-ehs)

Quatro 4 (cwah-trr-oh)

Cinco 5 (seen-coh)

Chinese

星期一 xīngqīyī **Monday**
(sin-chee-E)

星期二 xīngqīèr Tuesday
(sin-chee-R)

星期三 xīngqīsān Wednesday
(sin-chee-Sun)

星期四 xīngqīsì Thursday
(sin-chee-suh)

星期五 xīngqīwǔ Friday
(sin-chee-woo)

星期六 xīngqīliù Saturday
(sin-chee-lee-yah)

星期天 xīngqītiān Sunday
(sin-chee-T-N)

Japanese

こんにちは

konnichiwa

Hello

おげんきですか
o genki desu ka
How are you?

I'm fine.
私は元気です
Watashi wa genkides

nice to meet you.

はじめまして
Hajime-mashte

Tagalog

Magandang umaga
Good Morning.

Magandang tanghali.
Good noon

Magandang gabi
Good evening

Military time

Standard Time - 12 Hours	Military Time - 24 Hours
12:00 AM	0000
1:00 AM	0100
2:00 AM	0200
3:00 AM	0300
4:00 AM	0400
5:00 AM	0500
6:00 AM	0600
7:00 AM	0700
8:00 AM	0800
9:00 AM	0900
10:00 AM	1000
11:00 AM	1100
12:00 PM	1200
1:00 PM	1300
2:00 PM	1400
3:00 PM	1500
4:00 PM	1600
5:00 PM	1700
6:00 PM	1800
7:00 PM	1900
8:00 PM	2000
9:00 PM	2100
10:00 PM	2200
11:00 PM	2300
12:00 AM	2400

Morse Code

tap tap

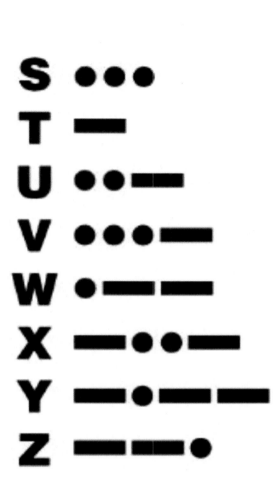

Thai

สวัสดี

(sah-waht-dee)
Hello/Good-bye

สบายดีไหม

(sah-baai-d-my)
How are you?

สบายดี

(sa-baai-dee)
I'm fine.

赤　橙　黄

Japanese

緑　藍　紫

Aka (ah-kah) Red	**Daidaiiro** (dye-dye-e-roh) Orange
Kiiro (key-rroh) Yellow	**AO** (ah-oh) Blue
Murasaki (moo-rah-sah-key) Purple	**Midori** (me-doh-ree) Green

Hebrew

Shalom

Ahlan

אַהְלַן

Hello

Ma nishma?

מָה נִשְׁמַע

How are things going?

Italian

**Buongiorno Buongiorno
sono Amore
Good morning Good Morning
I am Love**

uno 1 (uu-noh)
due 2 (do-eh)
tre 3 (trreh)
quattro 4 (kwah-trroh)
cinque 5 (seen-qweh)

Hebrew

שלום

Achat 1

Shtaim 2

Shalosh 3

Arba 4

Hamesh 5

Korean

안녕하세요

(Ahn-young ha-seh-yoh)
Hello

이름이 뭐예요?

(ee-reum-ee mo-eh-yoh)?
What's your name?

만나서 반가워요.

(mah-nah-so pahn-gah-woh)
Nice to meet you.

Macedonian

Добредојдовте

(doh-breh-doy-dohf-day)

Welcome

Како се викате?

(kah-koh-seh-V-kah-teh)

What is your name

Јас се викам Amor...

(Yah-seh-V-come)

My name is Love...

Tagalog

isa 1
(E-sah)

dalawa 2
(dah-lah-wah)

tatlo 3
(taht-loh)

apat 4
(ah-paht)

lima 5
(lee-mah)

Spanish Song

Oh ¡Buenos Días! **Oh** ¡Buenos Días!
Let's sing Good Morning

Oh ¡Buenas Tardes! **Oh** ¡Buenas Tardes!
Let's sing Good Afternoon

Oh ¡Buenas Noches! **Oh** ¡Buenas
Noches!
Let's sing Good Night

Oh ¿Cómo tu tá? **or** ¿Cómo estás?
Let's sing How are you?

Oh Yo te quiero **or** Te Amo
Lets sing I love you

Oh ¿Cómo te llamas?
¿Cuál es tu nombre?
What is your name?

Sawubona

(sah-wuu-boh-nah)

I see you

me and my ancestors see you

Zulu

Latin

Quamdiu spirabo numquam despondebo

(kwahm-d-u spee-rah-boh newm-kwahm dehs-pohn-deh-boh)

As long as I breathe,
I will never quit

Thank You
English

¡Muchas Gracias!
Spanish

Спасибо

Russian

Xiè Xiè nin
Chinese

Merci beaucoup
French

Arigatou gozaimasu
Japanese

Namaste

(nah-mah-Steh)

"I bow to the divine in you."

Hindu

ASL

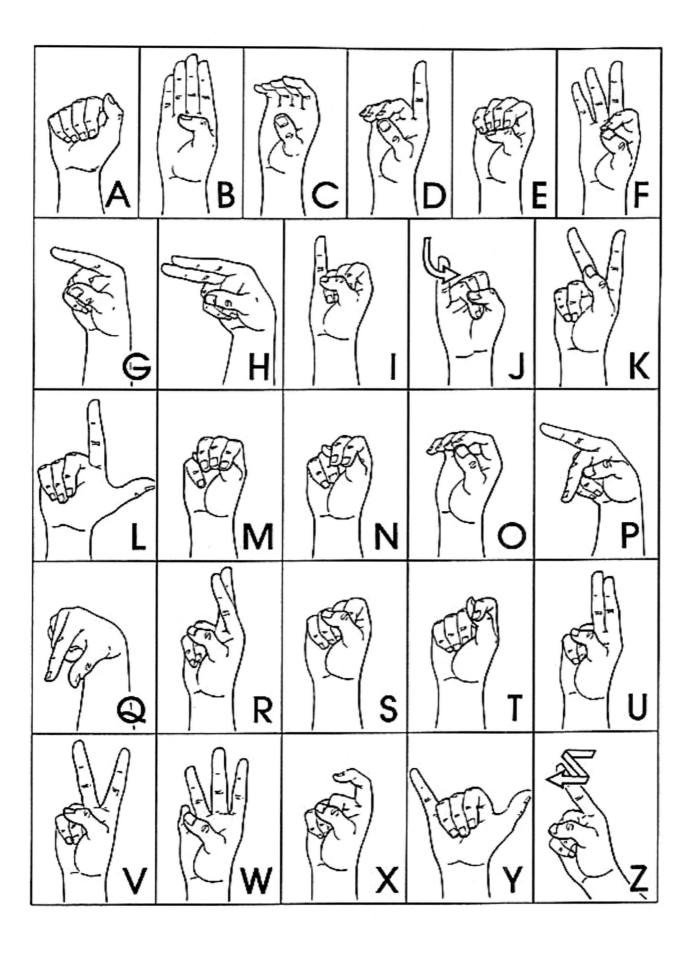

Mandarin Chinese Phrases

这是我们的商业计划

(zhè shì wǒ men de shāng yè jì huà)

This is our business plan

很高兴认识您

(Hěn gāoxìng rènshi nín)

I am very glad to meet you

Learn A Language 4 Fun, LLC
Bilingual Study Guides Available Now!

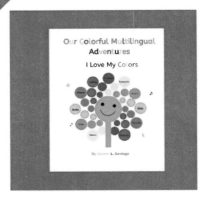

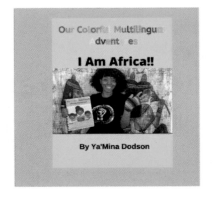

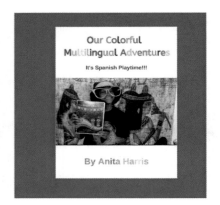

Shy Santiago (216) 217-8280
www.learnalanguageforfun.com